LAUGH WHEN YOU SAY, "I DO"

Cartoon and Jokes for Newlywed Folks

by Joel Rothman

Published by:
Humor House, Inc.
Flat 1
12 Ornan Road
Belsize Park
London, NW3 4PX
England

Phone: (44) 207-431-0873
Email: joelrothman@btconnect.com

©Copyright 2006 by Joel Rothman

ISBN: 978-1-930596-52-9

All rights reserved. No part of this book may be reproduced or transmitted in any form or by any means (electronic or mechanical, including photocopy, recording, or any information retrieval system) without the written permission of the publisher.

Distributed by:
The Guest Cottage, Inc
8821 Hwy 47
P.O. Box 848
Woodruff, WI 54568

Phone: 800-333-8122
       715-358-5195
Fax: 715-358-9456
Email: nancytheguestcottage.com

Dedicated
to my daughter, Andrea
and my son-in-law, Larry
who were brave enough
to take the plunge.

Just before the ceremony the groom was so nervous he could hardly talk straight. He told the bride's father, "I just want to thank you for your daughter's hole in handy matrimony."

She's lucky —— the groom is an archaeologist —— the older she gets the more interested he'll be in her!

Common marriage proposal —
"You're gonna have a WHAT?"

Puffed Rice —— what you throw at weddings when the bride is expecting.

Scientists have just proven there's one dessert that can lower your sex drive —— wedding cake!

I once got beaten up for kissing the bride after the ceremony — it was three years after the ceremony.

I'm waiting for Mr. Right,
but in the meantime I'm
going to marry Mark
on Sunday!

What nerve —— it cost me 50 grand to make the wedding, and here on the social page it says I gave the bride away!

The bride works as a waitress in that Shish Kebab Restaurant.

I heard she has a very bad case of anorexia.

The night of our honeymoon my husband took one look at my breasts and asked, "Are they all for me?"

Dolly Parton

Hollywood Starlets —— women who complain, "Always the bride, never the bridesmaid."

Bride —— a veiled threat.

No, you idiot ——
just because she's wearing
a veil doesn't mean she's
an Arab bride!

Did you hear about the male octopus who married the female octopus?
Together they walked down the aisle arm-in-arm-in-arm-in-arm-in . . .

My fiancé and I have a little problem. What I want is a church wedding with bridesmaids, flowers and no expense spared for the reception, meal and gown. What he wants is to marry another woman!

**The wedding was last week —
you'll just have to accept
that he's the man I
married, mother.**

Soon you and Jim will set the wedding date, so heed my advice — if you want him to remember your wedding anniversary, get married on his birthday!

Adore your new husband, trust your new husband, and get as much in your own name as possible . . .

**You've done a great job, Rudy —
I couldn't have found a better
best man.**

A secretary who worked in a busy office arrived one morning and began handing out big cigars tied with a blue ribbon.

"What's the occasion?" asked her boss.

She proudly displayed a new diamond engagement ring and announced, "It's a boy —— six feet tall weighing 180 pounds!"

I'm against gay marriage —
I think marriage is a sacred
union between a man and a
pregnant woman!

We're anxious to have grandchildren. Our boy is having his wedding next week, but we don't feel we're losing a son —— we just think we're gaining a uterus!

Weddings and marriages are not what they used to be.

No —— what they used to be were required!

I remember when a mother saved her wedding dress for her daughter. Today she has a daughter who saves her wedding dress for her next wedding!

Remember —— if you ever have an argument don't keep him in the doghouse for too long or he's liable to give his bone to the woman next-door!

The horse you bet on
came in at 30-1 so your
day hasn't been a
total loss!

**Don't expect the first year's meals to be great —
it takes time to find the right restaurants!**

We're still newlyweds — we've been married for exactly 19 frozen dinners!

Years ago we had a very posh wedding —— they even had a figure of my wife carved in ice —— it turned out to be a prophecy!

Don't cry dear —— after all we're not losing a daughter, we're gaining a bathroom!

The wedding came to an end and they lived happily *even* after.